Mythical Beasts

By Andrea Mills

Editors Katy Lennon, Kritika Gupta
US Editors Shannon Beatty, Megan Douglass
Project Art Editors Emma Hobson, Yamini Panwar
Art Editor Roohi Rais
Jacket Coordinator Francesca Young
Jacket Designer Suzena Sengupta
DTP Designers Dheeraj Singh, Nand Kishor Acharya
Picture Researcher Sakshi Saluja
Illustrator Dan Crisp
Producer, Pre-Production Dragana Puvacic
Producer Barbara Ossawska
Managing Editors Laura Gilbert, Monica Saigal
Managing Art Editor Diane Peyton Jones
Deputy Managing Art Editor Ivy Sengupta
Delhi Team Head Malavika Talukder
Creative Director Helen Senior
Publishing Director Sarah Larter

Reading Consultant Linda Gambrell
Educational Consultant Jacqueline Harris

First American Edition, 2018
Published in the United States by DK Publishing
345 Hudson Street, New York, New York 10014

Copyright © 2018 Dorling Kindersley Limited
DK, a Division of Penguin Random House LLC
18 19 20 21 22 10 9 8 7 6 5 4 3 2 1
001–310459–Oct/18

A catalog record for this book is available from the Library of Congress.
ISBN: 978-1-4654-7727-9 (Paperback)
ISBN: 978-1-4654-7728-6 (Hardcover)

Printed and bound in China.

The publisher would like to thank the following for their kind permission to reproduce their photographs:
(Key: a-above; b-below/bottom; c-center; f-far; l-left; r-right; t-top)

3 Dreamstime.com: Breakermaximus (br). **5 Dorling Kindersley:** The University of Aberdeen (bl, c, br). **7 akg-images:** Roland & Sabrina Michaud. **8-9 Alamy Stock Photo:** Ivy Close Images. **10-11 123RF.com:** Lorelyn Medina. **12 Dorling Kindersley:** Newcastle Great Northern Museum, Hancock (bl). **13 123RF.com:** Anton Tokarev. **14 Science Photo Library:** Jamie Chirinos (clb). **15 Bridgeman Images:** Pictures from History / Woodbury & Page (cra). **Getty Images:** Nigel Pavitt (cb). **iStockphoto.com:** VeraPetruk (cla). **Rex by Shutterstock:** Nathan Anderson (crb). **18 Alamy Stock Photo:** Witold Skrypczak. **Dreamstime.com:** Alinamd (Clouds). **22 123RF.com:** Rafael Ben-Ari (bl). **23 123RF.com:** Richard Whitcombe (br). **Alamy Stock Photo:** World History Archive (tr). **TopFoto.co.uk:** Ullsteinbild (cl). **25 Alamy Stock Photo:** Sabena Jane Blackbird. **26-27 iStockphoto.com:** MadKruben. **28-29 123RF.com:** Tawatchai Prakobkit. **30-31 Alamy Stock Photo:** The Granger Collection (b). **31 Dreamstime.com:** Breakermaximus (c). **32 123RF.com:** Vera Petruk (cl). **Dreamstime.com:** Luca Oleastri (br). **33 Alamy Stock Photo:** William Brooks (clb). **Dreamstime.com:** Restavr (r). **34-35 Depositphotos Inc:** Russian-photo. **36 Alamy Stock Photo:** North Wind Picture Archives. **38-39 123RF.com:** pbqhf427. **40-41 Alamy Stock Photo:** Science History Images. **44-45 123RF.com:** Vilainecrevette. **44 Getty Images:** DEA / G. Nimatallah / De Agostini (cr). **45 Alamy Stock Photo:** Ivy Close Images (tl); Matthew Wight (bl). **47 123RF.com:** Maksym Shevchenko. **49 Corbis:** Ocean. **50-51 123RF.com:** Shihina. **54 123RF.com:** Iosif Lucian Bolca. **55 123RF.com:** Lakhesis (t); Panu Ruangjan (cla). **Dreamstime.com:** Javarman (cra). **57 123RF.com:** Eric Isselee (cla). **Dorling Kindersley:** Canterbury City Council, Museums and Galleries (clb). **Getty Images:** SSPL (crb). **59 Alamy Stock Photo:** Science History Images. **63 iStockphoto.com:** Chuvipro

Endpaper images: *Front:* **Alamy Stock Photo:** North Wind Picture Archives; *Back:* **Alamy Stock Photo:** North Wind Picture Archives

Cover images: *Front:* **Dreamstime.com:** Chorazin3d b; **iStockphoto.com:** Breakermaximus crb, egal; *Back:* **Dreamstime.com:** Breakermaximus cl

All other images © Dorling Kindersley
For further information see: www.dkimages.com

A WORLD OF IDEAS:
SEE ALL THERE IS TO KNOW
www.dk.com

Contents

4 Introduction

6 Chapter 1: Meet the Monsters

14 *Monsters Map*

16 Chapter 2: Flying Fiends

22 *Dragons*

24 Chapter 3: Earthy Creatures

32 *Local Legends*

34 Chapter 4: Water Wonders

44 *Spectacular Sea Creatures*

46 Chapter 5: Super Shapeshifters

56 *Total Tricksters*

58 Quiz

60 Glossary

62 Index

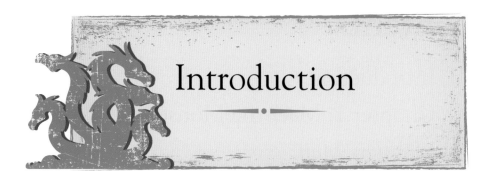

Introduction

Myth means tale or story. It comes from the Greek word "mythos." People have shared stories about mighty monsters and bizarre beasts since ancient times. These tales help people understand themselves and the world around them.

Myths have been retold over the years in art and music, as well as in stories. With each retelling, the content and creatures may change. As people move around, their myths and stories travel with them. This makes it very difficult to track where myths originally came from.

Turn the page and get ready to meet beautiful beasts, sneaky shapeshifters, and creepy critters. They are the things that legends are made of!

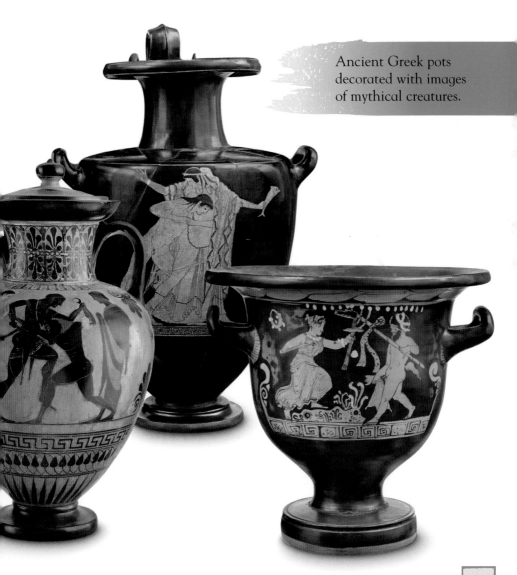

Ancient Greek pots decorated with images of mythical creatures.

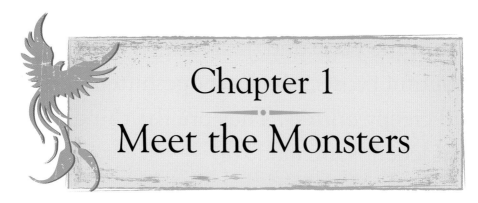

Chapter 1
Meet the Monsters

The most important creature in ancient Chinese mythology is Pan Gu. Born from a cosmic (space) egg, he had horns, tusks, and a hairy body. As the first living being, Pan Gu got to work creating the universe. He pushed the sky away from the earth by growing ten feet taller every day for 18,000 years. When Pan Gu died, his hair became the stars, his eyes became the sun and moon and his body parts were transformed into the rest of the universe.

Pan Gu was a believer in the two forces of yin and yang. These forces must be balanced for people to live in harmony.

氏古盤沌混

Enormous giants were the first beings on Earth in many cultures. The frost giant Ymir [ee-MEER] was the first in Norse (Viking) mythology.

The Norse world formed when fire and ice collided. This made the ice melt into water, creating Ymir. As more giants appeared, the gods grew scared of them. Ymir was killed and the gods used his body parts to make the landscape.

Ymir, the first being, was the father of all giants.

His hair became trees, his skull the sky,
and his brain formed clouds. His bones
made mountains and his blood flowed as
seas. A wall between the gods and giants
was built from Ymir's huge eyebrows.

A fantastic, flapping firebird called a phoenix is featured in the legends of ancient Greece and Egypt. The song of the phoenix was so beautiful that the sun god would stop his chariot just to listen to it.

Toward the end of its life, the phoenix was thought to build a special nest. It set the nest on fire before being reborn from the ashes. The new phoenix flew up to the sky to give the gift of an egg to the sun god. This magical bird is a symbol of long life, rebirth, and eternal hope.

It is believed that phoenixes can live for up to 500 years.

Beware the grotesque Gorgons! Anyone who stares at these scary snake-haired sisters will be instantly turned to stone.

These ancient Greek women had vast wings, sharp fangs, and scaly skin. The most famous sister was Medusa. She was cursed with slithering snakes on her head after claiming her hair was more beautiful than a goddess's. Medusa met a dire end when the Greek warrior Perseus set out to slay her. Using a bronze shield as a reflective mirror to avoid her gaze, Perseus cut off Medusa's head. He became a hero.

Bronze shield

Medusa was the only Gorgon who could be killed.

Monsters Map

Planet Earth has always been a monster's playground. Be brave as you travel far and wide to trace the origins of these memorable monsters!

Ymir—Scandinavia (see pp.8–9)

NORTH AMERICA

Ninki Nanka—Gambia

This swamp monster has the body of a crocodile with a giraffe's neck and a horse's head.

SOUTH AMERICA

El Chupacabra—Puerto Rico

This monster is a mix of lizard and coyote. Its legend grew from stories of beasts in Mexico and the USA.

Cerberus—Greece
Known as the hound of Hades, this three-headed dog stood guard outside the Underworld to keep the dead from escaping.

Ushi-oni—Japan
The water-dwelling Ushi-oni has an ox's head. Its body is made of parts from different animals, including a spider, cat, and crab.

Medusa—Greece
(see pp.12–13)

EUROPE

ASIA

Pan Gu—China
(see pp.6–7)

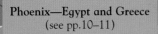

Phoenix—Egypt and Greece
(see pp.10–11)

AFRICA

Yara-ma-yha-who—Australia
The yara-ma-yha-who is small in size and has suckers for fingers. Its skin is bright red.

AUSTRALIA

Garuda—India
The king of the birds has an eagle's head, wings, and claws, with a human body. He punishes wrong-doers by eating them.

Chapter 2
Flying Fiends

The great griffin is part of mythology across Europe, Asia, and beyond. It has the beak and wings of an eagle and the body of a lion.

Griffins were considered the most majestic mix of creatures. With super strength, they have been described as more powerful than 12 eagles and more dangerous than a pride of lions. Griffins were strong enough to snatch up horses and their riders in their talons. They were also guardians, trusted to protect gold and other treasures.

Their strength and leadership meant they were pictured on the shields of medieval knights.

Griffins were believed to build their nests from gold.

A thunderbird totem pole in Victoria, British Columbia, Canada.

Native American tribes tell tales of the Thunderbird. They celebrate it in carvings and totem poles. However, sightings and stories of the Thunderbird have always struck fear into human hearts.

When this monstrous bird took flight the sky would fill with thunderstorms. Thunderclaps came from each flap of its wings and lightning strikes from each blink of its eyes. The Thunderbird was so large that it could grab whales out of the ocean and carry them away to eat.

Arabian legends tell of a winged terror called the Roc. It features in a classic Arabian story, *One Thousand and One Nights*. It also appears in the traveler's tales of Italian adventurer Marco Polo.

According to one story, this eagle-like bird could even carry off elephants.

Seeing the Roc meant a failed harvest or bloody battle was on the way. The Roc had a huge hunger to match its size. It could grab its prey in its enormous claws. Rocs were thought to be able to snatch whole ships from the sea.

Dragons

The history of dragons is a tale of two continents. Flying, fire-breathing dragons were feared in Europe. Slinky, serpentlike dragons were thought to be lucky in Asia.

Kuh Billaur
In ancient Persia, there was an evil dragon called Kuh Billaur. He was killed by the sword of the hero, Ali.

Gargoyle
Instead of fire, French dragons, called gargoyles, squirted water. Gargoyle sculptures were put on buildings to scare away enemies.

Ryu

This snakelike dragon hid beneath the ocean in Japan. He created terrible storms. However, those who faced the creature would have their wishes granted.

Fafnir

In Scandinavian myth, a dwarf named Fafnir was turned into a fire-breathing dragon. He was killed by the dragon-slayer, Sigurd.

Komodo

The only dragon alive today is the Komodo dragon. It is the largest living lizard. Komodo dragons live in the volcanic islands of Indonesia.

Chapter 3
Earthy Creatures

An elephant never forgets, and Indian stories always remember the jumbo Airavata. This special elephant is easy to spot as it has five trunks and ten tusks. The Hindu god Brahma crowned Airavata King of the Elephants.

In Indian mythology, Airavata is known as "elephant of the clouds," because he gave the world water. Airavata made rain clouds form above Earth. He sucked up water with his trunks and sprayed it into the sky.

Mural of Airavata at a temple in Thailand.

The most magical of mythical creatures is the unicorn. This white horselike creature has a single twisted horn on its head. Touching the horn can heal people and bring good luck. Legend has it that if the unicorn dips its horn in water, the liquid instantly becomes pure.

The myth of the unicorn is found in many different countries. European stories describe it as a wild and free-roaming creature. Asian tales say that it has a shy and sweet nature. Some people claim that sightings of unicorns are really just other horned animals.

Some cultures believed that unicorn horns could be used to detect poison.

The Haechi [hay-CHAI] of Korea is a monstrous mix of lion and dog. People thought that it liked to eat children! It was also thought that Haechi could swallow fire and would always punish those who did evil deeds.

Haechi has become a symbol of protection. Many buildings in Korea have statues of Haechi at their entrances. People think that the stone watchdog will protect buildings from fire and other disasters.

A Haechi statue at the Gyeongbokgung Palace in South Korea.

Make way for the mighty master of mazes—the Minotaur! This ancient Greek monster combined a human body with the head and tail of a bull. King Minos of Crete ordered the construction of a maze, so that the Minotaur could be locked inside, unable to escape. People were sacrificed to feed the bull-headed beast.

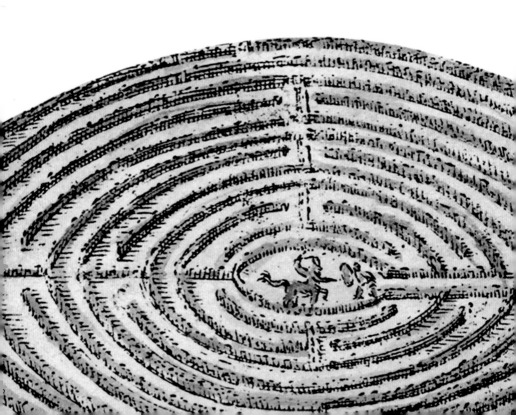

The Greek hero Theseus didn't agree with this and took revenge on the Minotaur. He entered the maze and killed the Minotaur in a deadly duel.

Minotaur

Theseus and the Minotaur fighting in the maze.

Local Legends

There have been many reported sightings of creatures from myths. Here are some of the most famous ones.

Yeti

Hairy and scary, the Yeti lives high in Asia's Himalayan Mountains. Climbers have reported seeing this apelike animal. However, its existence has never been proved.

Mothman

This flying figure haunted Point Pleasant in Virginia, USA, in the 1960s. People reported seeing a man-sized bird with devilish red eyes.

Beast of Bodmin Moor

In England in 1995 there were many sightings of a black panther with scary white eyes. The government investigated but no evidence of the beast was ever found.

Bigfoot

Bigfoot is the Yeti equivalent in North America. This forest dweller is also known by its Native American name, "sasquatch."

A footprint that is believed to be Bigfoot's was found at the Rouge National Urban Park, Canada.

Chapter 4
Water Wonders

A Scottish lake, or loch, is home to one of the world's most famous monsters—the Loch Ness Monster. The lake is deep, dark, and mysterious, the perfect home for the shy beast. People have described it as a long-necked, dinosaur-like creature up to 30 ft (9 m) long.

Sightings increased when a road was built next to the loch in the 1930s. Hundreds of photographs taken by monster spotters were later proved to be fake. Experts searched the waters of Loch Ness using sonar and cameras. However, even this special equipment found nothing. There is no proof the Loch Ness Monster exists, but people still claim to have seen her.

No one has been able to prove that the Loch Ness Monster exists.

The Kraken may have been a giant squid. Giant squids can grow up to 50 ft (15 m) long.

In the sea near Norway and Greenland lurks a super-sized sea monster called the Kraken. The legend goes that sailors thought the Kraken was an island. When they got closer, the Kraken grabbed hold of their ships. Whole crews were pulled underwater.

When near the surface, the Kraken was very dangerous. It could cause just as much trouble when it swum down to the seabed. It could suck the seawater down and around, causing a deadly whirlpool.

Many people say the Kraken never existed. They suggest sailors were more likely to have spotted real-life sea creatures, such as giant squid or huge octopuses.

Water demons are said to live in the depths of lakes and rivers in Japan. For centuries, kappas have hidden underwater, waiting to cause problems. Most reports describe them as scaly green imps the size of young children. Kappas' heads have dents in them, which fill with water and give them special powers.

Some people think kappas are naughty little imps playing harmless tricks. They are often described as being very polite. If you bow to them they will bow back. This makes them spill the water from their heads and lose their powers.

Kappa statues next to a pond in Japan.

Greek myths tell of a many-headed serpent that hid under the surface of Lake Lerna. It was called the Hydra and its foul breath polluted the water. If one of its heads was chopped off, more grew back in its place.

The Hydra was killed by a Greek hero called Hercules. This fearless warrior sliced off the Hydra's heads one at a time. He then quickly burned the necks, so no more heads could grow back.

The Hydra was snakelike, with many heads.

Throughout history, sailors have talked about creatures with the head, body, and arms of a human, and the tail of a fish. They are called mermaids and are beautiful but dangerous. They should never be approached and their sweet songs mean trouble.

People believe that mermaid's songs lead ships off-course, making them crash into rocks and sink. Seeing a mermaid means that you could drown. Mermaids are also thought to call sailors down to the bottom of the sea, never to return.

Some myths suggest that mermaids knew what would happen in the future.

Spectacular Sea Creatures

There are many stories of sea creatures that are part human and part animal. Here are some of these creatures who like to make a splash.

Triton
Like a mermaid, Triton has a man's head, chest, and arms, with the tail of a fish. A messenger of the sea in Greek mythology, he used seahorses to travel through the waves.

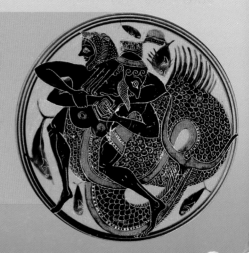

Sirens

The scariest sound in the sea is the call of the Sirens. These deadly women from Greek mythology use their magical music to lure sailors to them, then drown them underwater.

Sobek

With gigantic jaws and an appetite to match, this Egyptian god has a man's body with a crocodile's head. Ancient Egyptians worshipped him, but were also terrified of him.

Kelpie

In Celtic mythology, this water horse roams the seas of Scotland. It can also take a human form. Kelpies are devious creatures and are best avoided!

Chapter 5
Super Shapeshifters

Legend has it that some cursed people transform into terrifying wolves in the light of the full Moon. They are called werewolves and they eat humans! Werewolves are human by day but wolf by night. They can only be stopped if they are shot with a silver bullet or arrow.

Werewolf stories began in medieval times, when wolves lived in the woods near people's homes. In areas without wolves, similar stories were told about shapeshifting bears and lions.

Werewolves look like a
mixture of humans and wolves.

Watch out, coyotes on the prowl! These wild dogs stalk the plains of North America. The trickster Coyote, who can change into human shape, is the hero of many tales told by Native American people.

One story tells how Coyote was chosen by the first humans to be the moon. He couldn't resist spying on the people below.

In another story, Coyote was the child of the sun and the moon. He helped make the animals, birds, and plants, and shape the first people from clay. Coyote often got into trouble by being boastful or foolish.

Real-life coyotes live all over North America.

Japanese cultures warn of big-nosed, red-faced demons called tengu. Tengu means "heavenly dog." These semi-human creatures have all kinds of special gifts. They have super strength, magical powers, and can fly.

Tengu have red faces and birdlike features, such as feathers.

Hiding out in wooded mountainsides, tengu are very good at being bad. They use fans to make wind and fly away with people they have kidnapped. Tengu also enjoy starting arguments and making problems.

Púcas were very clever,
and known for their
naughty schemes.

Irish legends talk of little creatures called Púca, which means "goblin." Scary Púcas are hard to spot because they can take on many different forms. Across Ireland, they are described differently. Some stories feature a golden-eyed horse. Other stories describe a goat-headed human.

Whatever shape a Púca takes, it is always best avoided. This is because the Púca brings doom and disaster.

Always up to mischief, Púcas enjoy telling stories and will often bend the truth. They enjoy talking with humans that they meet. However, their words can't always be trusted!

The most famous shapeshifter is the vampire. This monster can appear as a person with sharp fangs, a flying bat, or a chilling mist. Vampires bite people's necks and drink their blood. The ancient vampire Prince Vlad of Romania enjoyed putting human heads on sticks outside his creepy castle.

Bran Castle in Transylvania, Romania, is also called "Dracula's Castle."

In 1897 Bram Stoker made vampires famous with his book *Dracula*. The story tells of a creepy count who lives in a castle in Transylvania.

There are a few things that vampires are scared of. These are mirrors, garlic, and sunlight. A wooden spike through the heart is the best way to make sure that a vampire won't rise again.

Total Tricksters

Tricksters are mythical masters of mischief and mayhem. They all share a naughty streak and can bring a touch of comedy to ancient legends and folklore.

Anansi

The Ashanti people of West Africa tell tales about the spider trickster, Anansi. He is very clever and cunning.

Hare

This trickster is known in the USA as Brer Rabbit. He is quick-thinking and good at outsmarting other creatures.

Raven

In Native American legends, this busy bird enjoys planning pranks. He is famous for hanging the sun and moon in the sky.

Maui

Known as Maui-of-a-thousand-tricks, Polynesian hero Maui is a fisherman. His best catch is the North Island of New Zealand!

Bes

Egyptian entertainment came from this cheeky little god. Bes always stuck out his tongue when faced with danger.

Eshu

Tricky to spot, West African mischief-maker Eshu could appear as anything from a giant to a tiny boy.

Quiz

1 In Norse mythology, what was used to build the wall between the gods and the giants?

2 What gift did the phoenix give to the sun god?

3 Which classic Arabian story features the Roc?

4 In Indian mythology, what is Airavata known as?

5 Which mythical beast stands guard outside buildings in Korea?

6 Which creature's head does a Minotaur have?

7   What will a kappa do if you
    bow to it?

8   What happens if you stare
    at a Gorgon?

9   What does Tengu mean?

10 Where would you find
    El Chupacabra?

11 Which Egyptian god has a man's
    body and a crocodile's head?

12 What is the name of the spider
    trickster from West Africa?

Answers on page 61

Glossary

Continent
large area of land that has many countries on it, for example, Asia or Europe

Duel
fight or conflict between two people or groups

Equivalent
when two things are equal

Grotesque
something that is so unpleasant it becomes shocking or upsetting

Loch
large area of water in Scotland

Majestic
beautiful or impressive

Medieval
from or relating to the Middle Ages, a time in European history between the years of 600 and 1500

Polynesian
from or relating to Polynesia, a group of islands in the Southern Pacific Ocean